Estrangement of Parents

by Their Adult Children

by Sharon Waters

Estrangement of Parents
by Their Adult Children

by Sharon Waters

ISBN-13: 978-0692882153

ISBN-10: 0692882154

First Edition, 2017

Published in USA

For the grandchildren
and my grandmothers, who taught me
what is most important

Estrangement of Parents
by Their Adult Children

Contents

1. Why Estrangement, Why Now?

Shakespeare wrote about it in *King Lear*. A parent's relationship with their adult children can change, and it may not be what the parent expected; an adult child may change her interpretation of her childhood and subsequently reject a parent. It's an old story, but it never ceases to come as a shock to a newly estranged parent and unfortunately, it is becoming an epidemic.

The current epidemic may have started with the writings of Ayn Rand, but how her unchristian doctrine could take hold in a predominantly Christian culture is a mystery. Rand supported ethical egoism in place of altruism. Her philosophy of "rational self-interest" and her argument that selfishness is a virtue was formed in her 1940s and 1950s writings, and then took the 1980s "greed is good" generation by storm. Her philosophy's impact on politics and economics has taken its place in history, but beyond that, we are experiencing an influence on personal attitudes and family relationships in contemporary society.

The divorce rate, reported to be near 50 percent, is

1

certainly high in the US. One consequence is that PAS (Parental Alienation Syndrome), where one parent turns children against the other parent, is now legally recognized. But another alienation or estrangement has become more prevalent and not just in the U.S.—that of adult children who turn against older parents and refuse to have a relationship with them. It's not clear what has driven the epidemic of severed parent/adult child relationships, but the emphasis on self-interest is likely a contributing factor, if not key.

Estrangement has become recognized as a phenomenon that crosses all borders, cultures, and social strata. In a nation noted for its reverence and care of elders, even the Chinese have experienced their share of it. They responded by legally mandating that adult children attend to their parents' financial and social/emotional needs. Where social, cultural, or religious dictates have fallen by the modern wayside, legal action or state welfare is increasingly expected to pick up the slack.

What is causing the epidemic of estrangement between family members hasn't been under enough investigation to have confirmed key factors, but parents estranged by their adult children who communicate among themselves are discovering consistent factors and common ground.

****

2. Parents Rejected by Their Adult Children Find Common Ground

A striking parallel is that the estrangement comes out of the blue. In retrospect, there may have been signs, but never to the extent that parents would anticipate this rejection. Up until the point of estrangement, both parent and child would have evaluated the childhood experience in similar terms—it was typically good, or at least O.K. Then gradually, or more often suddenly, the adult child severs the relationship with the parent for no understandable reason to the parent. Parents can be anywhere on the social scale—divorced, happily married, rich or poor, educated or not so much. They can be addicts or models of parenthood. But every estrangement regardless of family history or circumstances leads to the same result. Adult children suddenly decide their parent has abused them to the point that their only recourse is to break off all relationship. They abandon the parent and deny grandchildren a relationship with their grandparent. This is called Estrangement or Alienation of Parents by Adult Children, and it's far more common than most realize.

What factors can explain this? Economic pressures and the social structure of modern families could contribute to it. Adult children who are now parents increasingly juggle jobs outside the home, volunteering, extracurricular busyness, lessons, and social events. "Helicopter parents" shuffle themselves and their children between obligations and activities. Everyone is constantly occupied and meals are often eaten separately as outside activities absorb the family's time. "Quality time" occurs in those rare moments that have gone unscheduled. Fitting in the elder parents becomes a burden; one of the first things an about-to-be-estranged grandparent will hear from their adult child is "I'm busy."

Adult children become more focused on friends and spouses for feeling connected through work, activities, and their marriages. Life is more about fun or self-achievement, less about duty and responsibilities beyond their immediate friendship circle or family. A spouse who is jealous about time, affection, or resources invested in their partner's parent has a solution in encouraging estrangement.

Need we mention electronic devices, the Internet, and social media? While adult children rush from one thing to the next, cell phones and laptops are attached to their hip. Electronic devices of every make and model have made adult children reliant on social media for news, companionship, entertainment, solace, and the "wisdom" needed for coping with contemporary life. The wisdom of elders to enlighten and guide younger generations has gone by the wayside.

The decreased dependency on extended family should be a major focus of study in the phenomenon of estrangement. Families are less rooted to communities; family members are not as dependent on each other for social and economic needs. Where family ties are less essential, they are more readily discarded.

****

3. The Language of Estrangement, Toxic and Apologies

In the language of estrangement, one overworked term stands out: Toxic. It is used everywhere and applied to everything that is perceived negatively—politically, socially, in the media, in a multitude of self-help books, and in blogs and articles. From a term originally used to describe harmful substances, it is now applied to individuals and to relationships. It has a double edge of ills. The person it's applied to is deemed "bad," "hateful," and "purposefully hurtful." The person on the receiving end of this toxic individual's behavior claims unmitigated emotional suffering. The adult child claims that the parent is knowingly and willfully behaving in "toxic" ways and that the only choice is to create as much social and physical distance as possible. Separation—abandonment of the parent—is the only solution the adult child will consider.

The "toxic" parent is often declared mentally ill. Given the current inclination to put a psychiatric label on everyone, it's a slam-dunk to find one for disparaging an elder parent. The "mental illness" tag implies a negative behavior toward the adult child that can't be fixed by negotiation. The toxic parent is expected to admit to and endlessly apologize for their behavior even though the apology is not accepted. Apology is not demanded as a way to repair the relationship, but as a means to manipulate and control the parent.

Estranged parents talk of "walking on eggshells" with their adult children. They will admit to inadequacies and attempt to make conversations as non-offensive and pleasing to the adult child as possible in hopes of patching the relationship. It doesn't work, but it damages the self-image and mindset of the parent, who becomes an emotional captive of the adult child. The "wounded" adult child doesn't offer apology, either for past faults or for their role in instigating estrangement.

The adult child "made ill" feels they have relief from distressful symptoms (nervousness, anxiety, general malaise) only by complete separation from the parent. To feel "safe" and to feel "relief," the adult child is also compelled to separate their parent from the other family members. This includes keeping grandchildren from their grandparent and encouraging the alienation of other family members—siblings, aunts, uncles, and family friends. The adult child feels that rejecting the parent will help them achieve "wellness." An estranged parent confirms their "toxic behavior" through apology, is isolated from telling their version of events to the rest of the family, and is deemed too mentally ill to be believed, anyway.

The long-term consequences for the adult child are not yet known, but the pop psychology media and unhelpful counselors applaud the estrangement. Complete self-interest is encouraged, the elder parent is blamed, and the alienating of the grandchildren is accepted as justified. Honor thy Mother and thy Father is out the window; Self-Interest is in.

****

4. Contemporary Wisdom Puts the Child's Self-Interest and Self-Actualization Above All Else

I was told of a college application essay that targeted a parent, a mother. Mom had a lot on her plate as a single parent of three small children. Mom was sometimes depressed and less than perfect. The teenager described it in her college application essay as sweeping, unmitigated damage to her, an endlessly wounded child. It could have been useful to start a therapy dialogue, but as a college essay that should predict a successful transition to college life and academic success, it failed. All but one school rejected the application.

However, the high school counselor that reviewed the essay condoned and encouraged the student's victim point of view, saying it was best to "fully express herself" at every opportunity. The counselor did not suggest further counseling, nor guide the student to a more appropriate setting to air her issues. The fact that the single mom would foot the bill for the college education was not part of the conversation.

The mother was targeted as the person to blame and the

child became a "special person" (victim) whose outlook is a reflection of coping with a toxic parent. The soon-to-be-adult-child student gets the message that her mother's behavior is the background for her feelings and actions, and that her mother is solely responsible for the student's outlook on life.

****

5. Child Rearing, Dr. Spock, and Permissiveness

Victorian childhood was idealized as a happy time for youngsters, but strict upbringing rules were still applied. Through the World War II era, children were subject to "spare the rod and spoil the child" beliefs. But the child rearing gloves were off as the 1950s adherence to rules and rigidity yielded to a free-for-all in child rearing guidance a decade later. In a modern world where social norms were being challenged, the number of books offering the latest in child rearing advice sold every year rivaled the number of children born.

Dr. Benjamin Spock's book *Baby and Child Care,* first published in 1946, lead the way and was second only to the Bible in sales. Interpretations for raising children were as varied as the readers, but the core belief was clear. Children were becoming viewed as individuals with needs, rights, and feelings of their own rather than as "seen but not heard" members of the family. The post war parental mission was to raise a freely expressive child that would grow into a well-adjusted adult. No effort or expense was spared as children were showered with material goods, signed up for the best in educational opportunities, and granted wide open liberties to "do their own thing." Restrictions and punishments were reduced or banished; Honor thy Mother and thy Father became Honor thy Child.

The connection will need more study, but it's worth noting that the rise in estrangement has a parallel in childhood permissiveness and that allegiance to parents is no longer a given—it's expected to be earned and it's conditional. Filial love, responsibility, and support have become questionable and disposable without social consequence. At the same time, responsibility for the emotional health and actions of adult children has been placed firmly on parents whom they feel may have failed in their child rearing efforts.

Anecdotal comments on how it's worked out for today's youth come from every corner, and Geno Auriemma, coach of the University of Connecticut's women's basketball team, takes it from the nursery to the sports fields in his latest statement: "We hear so much and see so much of the coddled generation these days and especially in youth sports, where there is a focus on the 'me' culture...

"They're allowed to get away with just whatever, and they're always thinking about themselves," he states. "Me, me, me, me, me. 'I' didn't score, so why should I be happy?'" Self-indulgence, high expectations, and self-focus pervade youth and young adult culture.

****

6. *Gaslighting and Separate Realities*

Gaslighting is a term that evolved from a movie (*Gaslight*, 1944) where a woman is driven mad by her husband who, among other deceptions, turned down the lights but insisted that it was light as day. Gaslighting means twisting a person's sense of reality to the point of confusion and self-doubt. Don't believe what you perceive to be true—believe what I say is true. "Gaslighting" is a similar tactic applied to perception and family memory in estrangement cases. The adult child begins with a big lie, and then refuses to admit that they lied or even said it. They alternate between belittling and praise, separation and promises of connection, so the parent is confused while others are in the circle of family and friends are aligned against them. The target parent eventually becomes isolated and doubts her own mind.

The adult children describe a vindictive, hateful, parent who has harmed the child during the child's upbringing. The bewildered parent's view is that while they admit to imperfections and mistakes, there was love and caring at the core of their intentions and they profess love and caring

15

for years into the estrangement. Gaslighting by the adult child undermines the parent's credibility, shames and confuses the parent, and only after extended time breaks down the love for and will to reunite with the adult child.

In current parlance parents and the adult child have different "realities." The adult child sees the parent as intentionally harmful throughout the upbringing of the child although specifies are hard to come by. If there is parent/adult child conversation at all, the adult child states "you always" paired with a generality. These fabricated events run through the adult child's mind and are relayed to a therapist, family, or friends so frequently that they become a reality for the adult child—and a reality challenge for the parent.

From an estranged parent: "My ES (estranged son) told me of a time when we were all on vacation together. He claimed he had to take the grandchildren out of the house and away because I had taken drugs, broken up furniture, and finally passed out, and he wanted to protect them from discovering the incident. But I had never been invited to spend time with him on vacation, nor had such a thing remotely like it ever happened. How could this have been a real event? When I challenged it, he got angry and changed the the subject, but clearly was going to hold on to this story. I think it was a way to cast me as 'dangerous' and to justify the withdrawal of my access to the grandchildren."

It's impossible that both "realities" could be true,

16

however, the adult child won't agree to any negotiations. It's not reconciliation the adult child seeks, it's admission that the estrangement is warranted. The adult child's story is so convincing that it could easily sway a therapist, counselor, friends, or other family members. The sympathy and support in turn reinforces belief in the fabricated or falsely embellished story.

There is telling behavior while relating these abused childhood stories. Either consciously or unconsciously, the adult child who relates the abused childhood story will only talk with family members or friends who aren't likely to question their version. Often it's family members who don't have much contact and hear only the adult child's side. The adult child cautions them to likewise abandon the target parent, so the parent is in this way silenced. The estranged parent might suggest joint therapy, but the adult child refuses to commit to a level playing field of negotiation. The adult child who estranges holds the "family memory" that will determine the relationship and in that sense controls the whole family, not just the parent.

Legitimate reasons for an adult child to be estranged from a parent of course do exist, such as real physical and sexual abuse. There may also be understandable resentment against a parent who knew about it, but allowed the abuse. Severe neglect by a parent is another reason. But what is severe neglect? Many states have "filial responsibility" laws that require adult children to assume financial responsibility for basic care of an indigent parent who has raised that child. The adult child is deemed responsible if the parent has (in the language of Chapter 273, Section 20 of Massachusetts laws) provided food, clothing and shelter for a child except in a case where the parent has lapsed into "non support of a child for ten years or more." The legal definition recognizes that parents aren't perfect and can run into problems of their own that affect the raising of their children. By law, the parent owes a child a place to live, food, clothing, and access to education. Circumstances may interrupt care-taking, but as long as the parent has not truly abandoned the child for an extended time, they have fulfilled their obligation. One hopes for a lot more, but adult children who instigate estrangement allege that the parent didn't do enough, and knowingly, willfully, and selfishly put their own needs before the child to the point of exceptional emotional harm. In short, the parent failed and the only "healthy" resolution is to break off the relationship.

In these situations, adult children don't present visible scars. Their complaint centers around "you make me feel bad" or "I can't be around you for my own well-being." The specifics are few but can take the form of "you make me drink (abuse substances)." The reasons are hard to pin down or are hidden behind the silence of estrangement, but the estrangement is complete.

****

7. Psychiatric Labels—There's One for Everybody

Beyond "toxic," the adult child will often claim her parent is mentally ill. Like a dartboard, the parent will be the target of psychological labels. Bipolar is the diagnosis du jour, followed by the old favorite, borderline. True mental conditions such as schizophrenia are mixed in with a litany of "personality disorders" that could cover just about anyone with whom they are having a problem.

It's worth noting how subjective mental diagnoses are. The original seven recognized mental disorders were defined by military psychiatrists tasked with putting a medical stamp on PTSD. From the original few, there are now well over 300 mental illnesses, emotional states, or character flaws that have been added to the bible of mental diseases, the *Diagnostic and Statistical Manual of Mental Disorders*, first published in 1968 and yearly since then. Without a physical link to any of these disorders, they are described and subjectively added to the manual by vote at the annual psychiatrists' conference. Patients in hospitals, clinics, and counselors offices are labeled, billing numbers for insurance claims are generated, and from there the disorders enter the popular media and pop psychology. The final stop can be with adult children searching for a way to justify estrangement from a "mentally ill" parent.

There is justification for describing and codifying mental disorders. An example is a patient who habitually talked and sang non-stop for three days, and then would fall asleep for 24 hours straight on the fourth day. He couldn't hold a job, had difficulty holding any relationship, was frequently hospitalized, and was diagnosed bipolar. Identification and treatment was warranted. But doctors should use caution diagnosing anyone bipolar who has "ups and downs," much less should adult children assign serious mental disturbances to parents they accuse of bad parenting.

A claim of emotional or mental disorder can be a way to undermine the parent's statements and point of view (their reality) while bolstering the adult child's claim of emotional abuse. A childhood that for all appearances was a reasonable one is redefined as deplorably flawed, leading to a need for parental estrangement. There is no sympathetic understanding for whatever parents faced. Rather than appreciation for having functioned and provided to the extent that they did, the parent gets a failing grade for child rearing and the ultimate in consequences— abandonment.

Adult children will enlist medical, psychiatric, and even law enforcement agencies, to further distance the relationship. The parent can be described as dangerous or in need of medical intervention in the form of hospitalization and drugs. The "mentally ill" parent is positioned so they cannot make a legitimate case for themselves; the preemptive adult child is believed, not the parent. \I

The adult child can take it to the extreme by instigating a court order for legal restraint. The parent is barred from making their case to family members, particularly the adult child and their immediate family, including grandchildren. Taking this extraordinary measure can further shame the estranged parent into silence. The parent can challenge restraining orders and have them overturned, but the distancing has been done. The adult child has signaled that they are in control of the relationship, completely and on their own terms.

Eventually the estranged parents may hurl the psychiatric darts back at the adult children. The selfishness of Narcissistic Personality Disorder is commonly directed at the adult children by their hurt and exasperated parents looking for a reason for the relationship breakdown. The narcissistic disorder "in which people have an inflated sense of their own importance, a deep need for admiration and a lack of empathy for others" (Mayo Clinic) seems to fit. Further, "behind this mask of ultra-confidence lies a fragile self-esteem that's vulnerable to the slightest criticism" makes sense to the parent who is walking on eggshells trying to maintain the relationship. Whether this is a mental disease, a personality disorder, a sign of our times, or a character flaw that's been with us since Narcissus saw his reflection in the pool, is up for grabs.

****

8. Adult Children Declaring Emotional and Physical Territory

Another form of distancing, besides claiming emotional and relationship territory, is by declaring physical territory. A neighborhood, a town or city, or perhaps even a state, can be declared off-limits to the parent. The adult child sets the limits, and informs the parent they cannot be in that location without permission—that it "belongs" to the adult child.

Regardless of whether the adult child is in communication with the estranged parent, the son or daughter stakes the territory claim. At some point, the physical boundaries are announced, and the parent is expected to comply for the adult child's "well-being."

****

9. The Estrangement Dynamic

There are consistent factors in the estrangement dynamic unlike a situation where severe, real, abuse has caused adult children to separate from a parent. While the adult child distances himself, there also is every effort to disempower, manipulate, and control the estranged parent. The parent's point of view, expectation of relationship, and "reality" are discredited as "crazy."

Family members, therapists, medical people and legal forces are enlisted to believe in and act on the adult child's will. In spite of this, the parent will profess love for the child, while the adult child rejects all overtures for reconciliation. The estranged parent will endure making endless apologies, but nothing will be acceptable to the adult child.

Image is important to the adult child, and they will go out of their way to cultivate their image as a blameless victim. They put themselves forward as particularly caring individuals, in contrast to the real dynamic of estrangement.

1. The adult child insists on the estrangement from the parent, not the parent from the adult child.

2. The parent is expected to apologize for all grievances the adult child has.

3. The adult child believes they are not responsible for improving the situation; they feel the parent should have been a better person.

4. The adult child takes complete control.

5. Grandchildren are withheld as instruments of bargaining and control.

6. Hurt is all about the adult child; hurt to the parent is ignored.

7. Estrangement is instigated by the adult child first, then non-negotiable complaints follow.

8. Adult children who estrange parents are image conscious and often cultivate their image as caring, nurturing, and empathetic individuals.

9. Adult children are content with their division and do not feel guilt or seek therapy except to confirm the need for estrangement. Devastated parents seek solace from wherever they can get it without feeling further demoralized.

10. Adult children claim relief and a sense of well-being. Estranged parents bury their grief in emotional and physical symptoms including depression, substance abuse, and suicide.

What is the adult child gaining in all this? Control of time and resources could be a contender. Adult children, especially those with their own young children, are working, sitting in commuter traffic, running to activities, or engaged with electronics and social media. Children are in day care, school, or with babysitters. Adult children chauffeur their children from one activity to the next and meet up with friends. What and where is quality time for adult children and their families when challenged by overburdened schedules? The stress of adding time for an elderly parent may push them beyond their tolerance. Estranging a parent may be the exchange for whatever time and energy is left in a complex and frenetically paced world.

The mass media paints an image of older adults that children may find stressful. Well-off seniors may be on the golf course or a cruise; but the the media portrays a specter of mental deterioration, Alzheimer's, physical limitations, and medical or housing care that will strain the adult child's budget or add pressure to their schedules.

Senior parents are losing the "wise elder" status formerly attributed to them and less often move into the adult child's home in their later years. They are no longer essential in transmitting life skills, wisdom, or social connection within the family. They have become dispensable in a world focused on electronic communication, mass media, materialism, and acquisition; self-gratification is encouraged and elders are seen as a burden.

****

10. *Aphorisms, Memes, Picture Quotes and Motivational Messages*

Cures for emotional hurts are a common topic for pop psychology web sites, blogs, and online articles. There is the daily dose of it along with advice on how much coffee or wine to drink, how to declutter your home and your life, what makes a real friend, or how to unwind after a busy day. A particularly popular notion is that of "letting go." A version of it is "if they have hurt you, leave them." This message below was taken from the Internet and is typical:

> **YOU ARE ALLOWED TO TERMINATE YOUR RELATIONSHIP WITH TOXIC FAMILY MEMBERS. YOU ARE ALLOWED TO WALK AWAY FROM PEOPLE WHO HURT YOU. YOU ARE ALLOWED TO BE ANGRY AND SELFISH AND UNFORGIVING AND YOU DON'T OWE ANYONE AND EXPLANATION FOR TAKING CARE OF**
> ## YOU.

The irony is that both sides of the estrangement divide

absorb and forward these "healing the hurt" messages to others in their situation. Estranged parents pick up on messages of letting go since they have to manage life when all efforts to reconcile with adult children have failed. For the adult children it sends a message that estrangement is the easy answer and that they can toss aside an inconvenient relationship without guilt, social stigma, or consequence. They might even expect a pat on the back. At best, it's a simplistic suggestion for a complex problem. At worst, these memes instigate adult children to estrange their parent.

Who comes up with these pearls of wisdom? Often they are sent from websites that promise to "Heal your emotions, sadness, self-esteem, relationships, and anxiety through [my] 'Psychic & Happy' online courses...Coaching, and Angel Readings." The reader often finds a group to join, a course to sign up for, or a product to buy—or at the very least they boost the author's readership and following.

A group promising to expand the reader's consciousness shared an article: "5 Reasons Not to Feel Bad About Cutting Toxic Parents Out of Your Life." The article states that: "Sometimes parents simply aren't the people we need them to be." Further, parents might have "had big plans for you, but you [can] chose to live your own life instead of the one they had in mind." The advice to this generation of adults is to dispense with your parents—

and don't feel guilty about it. Take our advice, not that of your parents.

Keeping it short and simple has its merits, such as in "Know Thyself" and "One Day at a Time." But today's plethora of aphorisms focuses less on self-examination and self-improvement and more on self-satisfaction in relationship. The problem behavior is assigned to the other person and "walking away" is the catch-all solution. It offers little in the way of understanding, and nothing in the way of compromise. For the estranged parent who desperately wishes to regain a relationship with adult children and their grandchildren, there is little choice but to move on. As an excuse to abandon what adult children consider "relationship clutter" with parents, "walking away" is their answer. Remarkably, adult children will ask the parents they have estranged to "respect" their decision to abandon them and deny them access to their grandchildren.

Self-interest to the point of ignoring hurt inflicted upon others has become acceptable, and parents aren't the only ones feeling it. *The New York Times* defines the recent phenomenon of "ghosting" as "ending a romantic relationship by cutting off all contact and ignoring the former partner's attempts to reach out." Dependance on electronic communication rather than personal meetings and lack of social consequences make distancing without cause or explanation—"ghosting"—as easy as not answering the phone.

Otherworldly salvation is no longer life's goal in this less religious age; centering resources and attention on the self is the goal. Self-focus has become the core value and it replaces the messages of traditional community and tribe.

****

11. Who Gets hurt?

Do the grandchildren get hurt? Of course they do. Common sense would indicate that believing a grandparent has been extraordinarily hurtful to your parent, and would be the same toward you, is a dark message. The child is not only deprived of the special love that grandparents give, but is also warned to be suspicious and fearful. When grandchildren do recognize a disconnect between a loving grandparent and what their parents have told them, it damages the child's ability to trust. Having been taught to reject, the grandchild could learn to repeat this behavior toward their own parent when they become an adult. Being estranged from loving grandparents can seriously hurt the child and affect their relationships in adult life.

From a client: "My grandson said he would like to visit me but my ED (estranged daughter, his mother) said 'sometime.' That 'sometime' went into years, and then just never happened. I don't know how that child deals with this perpetual disappointment."

There is an emotional death between the parent and the adult child. Invariably the next question is how similar is this to an actual death? Anecdotally it is reported as being worse. The course of grieving has similarities with some stages being painfully extended. For parents who have been estranged, never-ending rejection exacerbates the loss. Self-blame and shame join the mix, and the parents experience isolation rather than the comforting support of others.

The loss of a child is not expected. Parents generally assume that they will sacrifice much while raising their children, but that they will live out the rest of their lives surrounded by loving family. For them, estrangement erases their family and the most important goal of their life, parenthood, has been deemed a failure .

For parents, shock, disbelief, and lack of acceptance brim to the surface. With the hope of reconciliation, the painful period of adjusting to loss often spans years. The stage of anger is especially prolonged and it escalates, rather than dissipates. When blame and hurtful conversations are extended, it's particularly agonizing.

Parents who have been estranged by their adult children have shame, self-doubt, and insecurity, and often isolate further. They rarely talk about it to others although it is a silent stigma that influences every aspect of their lives. Predictable physical complaints follow the emotional wounds and suicidal thoughts are common.

Even in the rare cases of reconciliation, trust isn't naturally restored. When the only coping is for the parent to stop caring, can they ever get those feelings back again?

The emotional and physical harm to estranged seniors affects everyone. It's not hard to imagine what impact the stress, social isolation, and lack of family support has caused. Estranged parents suffer from anxiety and sleep disturbances, and they can be driven to substance abuse.

From the National Institute of Health: "Across the nation, geriatricians and other health and social service providers are growing increasingly worried about loneliness among seniors ... Their concerns are fueled by studies showing the emotional isolation is linked to serious health problems. Research shows older adults who feel lonely are at greater risk of memory loss, strokes, heart disease, and high blood pressure. The health threat is similar to that of smoking fifteen cigarettes a day, according to AARP. Researchers say that loneliness and isolation are linked to physical inactivity and poor sleep, as well as high blood pressure and poor immune functioning."

Familial estrangement is a worldwide silent epidemic. Less well known, less understood, and much less discussed than the physical and financial abuse of elders, estrangement impacts the senior parents, the adult children and their relationships, and especially the grandchildren who are separated from grandparents by their parents' words and actions. Silence, lack of knowledge, and lack of empathy are pushing a remedy too far into the future. By sharing their experiences, estranged parents are finding ways to cope. Hopefully increased understanding and action will turn around the estrangement phenomenon for the benefit of parents, their adult children, families, society, and especially for the grandchildren who will have to carry this burden forward.

****

Epilogue

As a teenager, I had the good fortune to spend summers with my grandmother, who lived in a small cottage on a lake. As she approached her eighties, her sight and her physical strength were failing. It prepared me for understanding where I would eventually end up myself and I paid attention to her wisdom about how to cope as health and the dynamism of younger life fades away.

One day I stepped into the lake to take a swim. My grandmother, diligently watching from her chair on the shore, warned me, "Please don't go out farther than you can stand, Sharon."

"Why not, Grandma? I'm a good swimmer. You know it."

"But if something happened, I couldn't save you. Think how I would feel."

I learned that ultimately, the only thing we can truly have under our control is empathy.

Printed in the USA
CPSIA information can be obtained
at www.ICGtesting.com
LVHW011530080824
787620LV00002B/433